D1138461

MINE SHAFT

Barbara Mitchelhill

Published in association with
The Basic Skills Agency

Hodder & Stoughton

A ME

Acknowledgements
Cover: Fred Van Deelen
Illustrations: Mike Bell

Orders: please contact Bookpoint Ltd, 39 Milton Park, Abingdon, Oxon OX14
4TD. Telephone: (44) 01235 400414, Fax: (44) 01235 400454. Lines are open
from 9.00–6.00, Monday to Saturday, with a 24 hour message answering
service. Email address: orders@bookpoint.co.uk

British Library Cataloguing in Publication Data
A catalogue record for this title is available from The British Library

ISBN 0 340 74324 7

First published 1999
Impression number   10 9 8 7 6 5 4 3 2 1
Year   2004 2003 2002 2001 2000 1999

Typeset by Fakenham Photosetting Ltd, Fakenham, Norfolk.
Printed in Great Britain for Hodder & Stoughton Educational, a division of
Hodder Headline Plc, 338 Euston Road, London NW1 3BH by Athenaeum
Press, Gateshead, Tyne & Wear.

About the play

The People
- **Harry**
- **Emma**

The Place
Deserted moorland.

What's Happening
Harry and Emma are walking on the moors. Harry is complaining that nothing ever happens on the moors. Just hills and more hills.

Harry   This is the last time
I come on holiday with Mum.
Next year,
I'm going to do what *I* want.

Emma   Shut up, Harry!
We've been walking for half an hour
and you haven't stopped moaning.

Harry   Well, why did we have to come here?

Emma   We came because of Aunt Sheila.
Mum wanted to take her
to nice places.

Harry   I don't call this a nice place.
Our hotel is the only thing for miles.
Just hills and more hills.

Emma   You know Auntie Sheila
and Mum grew up here.
That's why they wanted
to come back.

Harry   But most of the time
they're sitting in the hotel
drinking coffee.
We've got nothing to do.
Everything round here is
dead boring.
I'm fed up.

Emma   Shut up, Harry.
Listen.

Pause

It's a helicopter. Look!
Over there beyond that peak.
You don't expect
to see them round here.

Harry   Yeah. I can see it.
It's probably
taking a famous pop star
to a really interesting place.
Or maybe flying a millionaire
to his country house.
Some people have all the luck.

Emma	I don't think it's doing any of those.
	I think it's a police helicopter
	and it's going round in circles.
	It must be looking for somebody.
Harry	Then they're probably
	lost in these hills.
	I bet people
	are always getting lost round here.
	Anyway, it's going away now.
	They can't have found anybody.
	What time is it?
	I'm starving.
	Got any crisps?
Emma	Shhh!
Harry	What?
Emma	I can hear something.
Harry	You've got ears like a bat!
Emma	Can't you hear that dog barking?

Pause

Harry	Yeah. So what?

Emma   Why would a dog be barking
        out here
        – miles from anywhere?
Harry   I don't know.

Pause

Emma   That dog doesn't sound right.
        It doesn't sound happy, does it?
        Could it be trapped, do you think?
        Maybe it's fallen down a mineshaft.
        There are loads around here, you
        know.
        Mum said so.
Harry   Right. Come on then.
        Let's go and see if we can find it.
        At least it'll be something to do.

*They run across the hill
in the direction of the barking.*

Emma   Over there, Harry.
        There's an opening in the side of
        the hill.
        That's where the noise is coming
        from.

Harry You're right!
It looks like the entrance to an old mine.

Emma Yes. I can just read that notice.
It says
'The Old Shankly Mine.
Keep out.'

Harry Yeah. Look!
It's all boarded up.

Emma But some vandals have smashed it. See?
A dog could easily get in.

Harry So could I.

Leaning into the mine.

Here boy!
Come here.

Pause

THE
OLD SHANKLY
MINE
KEEP OUT

I think he's coming, Emma.
Yes, here he is!
Hello boy!
What were you doing in there?
Look he's wagging his tail.
He's OK.
He's not hurt.
I think he's just lost.

Emma Harry!
Listen!
Can you hear something
inside the mine?

Harry No.

Emma I can.
I can hear groaning.
I think there's someone in there.
Maybe it's the owner of the dog.
Come on.
Let's go in and look.

They go into the cave.

Harry Oh, it stinks in here!
It's dark, too.
Real spooky!

Emma Your eyes will soon get used to it.
Whoever is in here is in real pain.
Just keep going 'til we find him.
He can't be far away now.

Harry Emma!
Look!
Down there.
There's another passage
and I can see something.
I'm going down it.

Emma   All right, Harry,
           but don't do anything stupid.
           Careful how you go.
           It's narrow.
           I'll wait here.
Harry OK.
           But keep talking to me.
Emma   I will.
           Watch where you step.
           There are loads of loose stones
           on the floor.
           Can you see anybody yet?
Harry Yes! A man.
           He's here.
           He's flat on his back.

           Pause

           He looks like he's asleep,
           but he's groaning.
           I'll shake him and see if he
           wakes up.

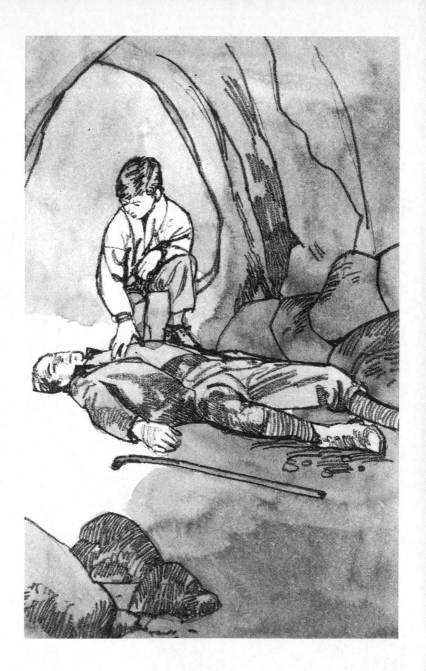

Emma	Careful!
	Not too hard, Harry.
	He might be injured.
Harry	Oh no!
	Yuk!
	Help!
Emma	What is it?
Harry	I've put my hand in this stuff!
	Er ... it's blood.
	It's all down his neck.
	I can feel it.
	Yuk! Yuk!
	I'm going to be sick.
Emma	Don't be stupid, Harry.
	We've got to help him.
	Let's get him out.
	He needs fresh air.
Harry	No.
	That's the last thing we should do.
	I think he's hurt really bad.
	We shouldn't move him
	We've got to get help.

Emma   Harry! Harry!
I can hear something.
I think the roof's falling in.
Get out of that tunnel!
Quick!
Run for it!

*Stones begin to fall and the entrance
to the small tunnel is blocked.*

Emma   (*screaming*)
Harry!
Can you hear me?
I'm trying to dig through to you
but ... it's ... too ... much.
I can't.
The stones are too big.
Harry!
Say something.
Are you all right?

Silence

Harry! Harry!

Silence

I've got to get help.
Somebody must come and
get them out.
You stay here, dog.
I need to be sure
where the mineshaft is.
Don't move.
I'm going up to the main road.
Maybe I can stop a car.

She runs up the hill to the road.

This must be
the loneliest road in the country.
Come on!
Come on, somebody.
Please!
Yes! At last! A car!
I'll wave.

No, I can't wait in the call box.
I've got to go back to Harry.

Pause

I don't care what you say!
I have to go back!

She runs back to the mine.

Hello boy!
Good dog!
Down boy!
I'm glad you're still here.
It's good to see you.

Harry (*coming out of the mine*)
Where've you been?

Emma Harry! I don't believe it.
How did you get out?
Wow! You look awful.

Hey! Stop!
I need help!
Stop!
Huh! Didn't even slow down.
Now what do I do?
I'll have to get to the nearest
village.
Maybe there'll be a house
along the way.
Let's hope so!

She starts running.

My luck's changed!
I can see a call box!

*She runs to the call box and dials
999.*

Please send help as quick as you
can.
My brother's trapped
in the Old Shankly Mine.

Pause

Hey! Stop!
I need help!
Stop!
Huh! Didn't even slow down.
Now what do I do?
I'll have to get to the nearest
village.
Maybe there'll be a house
along the way.
Let's hope so!

She starts running.

My luck's changed!
I can see a call box!

*She runs to the call box and dials
999.*

Please send help as quick as you
can.
My brother's trapped
in the Old Shankly Mine.

Pause

No, I can't wait in the call box.
I've got to go back to Harry.

Pause

I don't care what you say!
I have to go back!

She runs back to the mine.

Hello boy!
Good dog!
Down boy!
I'm glad you're still here.
It's good to see you.

Harry (*coming out of the mine*)
Where've you been?

Emma Harry! I don't believe it.
How did you get out?
Wow! You look awful.

Harry I don't feel too good.

(*coughs*)

My lungs are full of dust.
Emma You didn't answer when I called.
I thought you were hurt.
Harry I think I was knocked out
but when I came round
I pulled some of the stones away
and made a hole.
Anyway, where've you been?
Emma I went to get help.
I found a call box
and I called the police.
They're on their way.

Harry	Good.
	That bloke inside
	needs to go to hospital.
	His arm's broken and he's
	in a bad way.
	The noise of the rockfall
	brought him round.
	When I was digging my way out,
	he suddenly spoke to me.
Emma	Is he all right then?
Harry	He can't move but he can talk.
Emma	What did he say?
Harry	He told me his name was Tom
	Jackson.
	He was out walking his dog
	when he saw somebody
	breaking into the mine.
	He knew the mineshaft was
	dangerous
	so he ran in to warn him.
Emma	What happened?

Harry   The bloke who was in there
was a real thug.
He swore at Tom.
Told him to mind his own business.
Get lost.
He doesn't remember anything else.
I guess the thug beat him up
and left him for dead.

Emma   I'm pretty sure you're right, Harry.
That connects with
what the police told me
when I rang.

Harry   What do you mean?

Emma   They said
a man was on the run in this area.
He escaped from Harrington prison
this morning.
They set up a man hunt
to try and catch him.

Harry   That must be
what the helicopter was doing.
Looking for him.
If the bloke breaking into the
mineshaft
was the prisoner,
it explains a lot.
He was going to hide underground
so the helicopter couldn't spot him.

Emma   That makes sense.
The police said the man was
dangerous.
He was serving time for GBH.
They told me to wait in the call box
on the main road.
I'd be safer there
and they could easily find me.

Harry   But why didn't you do what they
said?
What if you'd met that thug?
He might have beaten you up!

Emma I know it was stupid
but I was worried about you!
I had to come back
– just in case
there was something
I could do.
I couldn't leave you alone.

Harry I wasn't alone.

Patting the dog.

You were right here
outside the mineshaft,
weren't you boy?

Emma (*laughing*)
The dog's not much help, is he?

Harry I guess not – but the police will be.
Listen. I can hear the sirens.
They'll be here any minute.

Emma Thank goodness.
Now we can get Tom to the hospital.

Harry   And we can get back to see Mum.
            Today turned out
            to be quite exciting, after all.
Emma   Yeah!
            A bit too exciting if you ask me.
            I can't wait to get back to the hotel
            for a bit of peace and quiet.